Upwardly
Mobile

SOUL SURVIVOR PRESENTS

Upwardly Mobile

HOW TO LIVE
A LIFE OF SIGNIFICANCE

DAVID WESTLAKE
WITH CRAIG BORLASE

Hodder & Stoughton
LONDON SYDNEY AUCKLAND

Copyright © 2000 David Westlake and Craig Borlase

First published in Great Britain in 2000

The right of David Westlake and Craig Borlase to be identified as the
Authors of the Work has been asserted by them in accordance with
the Copyright, Designs and Patents Act 1988.

10 9 8 7 6 5 4 3 2 1

British Library Cataloguing in Publication Data
A record for this book is available from the British Library

ISBN 0 340 75654 3

Typeset by Avon Dataset Ltd, Bidford-on-Avon, Warks

Printed and bound in Great Britain by
Clays Ltd, St Ives plc

Hodder & Stoughton
A Division of Hodder Headline Ltd
338 Euston Road
London NW1 3BH

'The greatest of evils and the worst of crimes is poverty.'

George Bernard Shaw, 1907

Contents

Contents

Foreword

Upwardly Mobile is the first in a series of books from Soul Survivor on crucial subjects aimed particularly at young Christians. This book is a fantastic start. I don't think I have ever read a book like it before.

It is both radical and prophetic, with insightful biblical teaching and also deeply moving illustrations and stories. David Westlake is currently Director of Youth for Tearfund and in that role has had to come to grips with the biblical commands to side with the poor and to uphold justice if we are truly to be Kingdom people.

David has written about these issues with both passion and humour and also with the integrity by which he is know. This is a balanced book. Usually when that is said about a book it actually means it is boring. This is balanced in the best possible way. David believes passionately in communicating the gospel in every way. We are to proclaim Christ with the words that we speak – whether preaching or personal testimony. We are to proclaim Christ with signs and wonders – the power of the Holy Spirit to bring healing and deliverance. We are also to proclaim Christ with works of compassion, love and grace, especially among the poor. *Upwardly Mobile* focuses on the works without belittling the words and the wonders.

This book moved me with its heart-rending and heart-warming stories of those who are spending themselves among the poor, the broken and the marginalised for the sake of Christ. It has also inspired and challenged me to do all I can to make a difference for the sake of the poor. Probably the major distinctive of Soul Survivor, the thing we are known for, is worship. We have rediscovered in the last few years that worship and justice go together. If we are to be a people of the Bible we must not separate them. When we feed the hungry, give drink to the thirsty, clothe the naked, visit the prisoner and welcome the stranger, we do it to Jesus. This is worship. David Westlake is a very godly man who has written a very 'godly' book. Reading it could change your life. I warmly commend it.

Mike Pilavachi
May 2000

Introduction

Every picture tells a story, and that on the inside cover is no exception. Oh dear. Why 'oh dear'? Well, the trouble with this little cliché is that we've all seen this kind of picture before. You know the sort of thing I'm talking about: another load of starving children, tummies swollen from malnutrition, hair turning a shade of copper due to vitamin deprivation; a column of refugees fleeing homes which have been ravaged by war or natural disaster, all they possess in the world being carried upon their backs. We all know these stories and, to be honest, we're bored with them. OK, so we might not be bored because we're spiteful (after all, we probably give what we can, putting coins in the collection or phoning up the operators in response to the Telethon); no, we're bored because we've seen it all too often. Every week we're confronted with new stories of desperate people whose lives have taken an even more desperate turn for the worse. We've seen so many of these pictures that we've lost the knowledge of what to do. After all, even with the gold star events like Live Aid and all those countless TV appeals, the pictures still keep on coming. We're left feeling helpless, worn down by too much déjà vu.

But if this picture was a little bigger you would see some other people. They're from the Evangelical Fellowship of Sierra Leone. These Christians at work in the refugee camp are digging latrines, dealing with people's sewage and sanitation so that they might know that there is a God in heaven who loves and cares for them. If you looked closely you would see Christians laying down their lives for people that the world has no time for.

If the picture was a little bigger still you would see someone else: Jesus. In Matthew 25 Jesus said that 'whatever you did for one of the least of these brothers and sisters of mine, you did for me' (v. 40). There he is, in the middle of this picture, doing what he always does: serving people, loving and blessing them. You see him? He's calling to you and me to come and meet with him in the middle of the poor.

We long for intimacy with God, and the Bible shows us three ways of discovering it. First, we can get closer to him through our praise and worship, our prayer and relationship with him. The second is by obeying him – as he said, 'those who love me will obey my commands'. The third way is this: finding him in the eyes and the lives of the poor.

This isn't going to be a heavy book about

poverty, one with a free guilt trip at the end of every chapter. Instead it is about intimacy with Jesus; being close to him, becoming like him. Next time you find yourself in front of one of these types of pictures on the TV, in a paper or magazine, don't flick the channel or the page; look a little more closely. Look and see brothers and sisters laying down their lives. See if you can find Jesus.

On a trip to Bombay with the charity I work for (Tearfund) I met a lady called Laishi. Having talked for a while about what she did and how we could continue to help her, she invited me to visit some friends. She took me to a slum on the edge of the city – a derelict area made up of once-grand Victorian warehouses that were now little more than rubble. People were living in the ruins of these old centres of commerce, having strung up scraps of corrugated iron and sheets to partition off areas for homes. She led me down a narrow alleyway, stepping over the human waste that flowed down between the rubble and playing children.

We arrived at a room no bigger than ten feet deep by eight feet wide, and I was introduced to

Laishi's friends. A woman stood at the front of the room, another older one (her mother-in-law, I later found out) was towards the back, and eventually my eyes made out a man lying on a mat on the left. He was feverish and obviously very ill. The lady at the back of the room was his mother, but was scared of coming too close to him as he was in the advanced stages of AIDS.

Laishi introduced us and the gentleman was embarrassed that in the presence of guests he was still on the floor. He struggled to get up, but it was too much for him and he began to cough and wheeze. Laishi immediately went over to him, knelt down and started to mop his brow. I just stood there feeling out of place. For want of something to say I asked the lady what her husband's name was. She started to tell me but broke down. Again Laishi was there to comfort her as she cried and cried and cried. She was dying of AIDS too, and her mother-in-law knew that one day she would have to take care of the children these two people would leave behind. I never did find out the man's name; he died the next day.

I felt embarrassed that I was intruding on this scene. Eventually Laishi suggested that we prayed. I prayed the best I could but I felt as though the words were just dribbling out of my mouth. When it was time to go I was relieved; I had felt so out of place in there. Walking out into the bright Bombay sunshine I was passed by the couple's twin daughters. They were three years old and had ran in to hug their mum. I looked back and the last thing I saw was Laishi still hugging the weeping lady as her two daughters held on to her legs. I remembered the words in the Bible: 'This is true religion: to visit the widows and the orphans and to keep yourself spotless from the world. This is true religion: to visit the outcast and the suffering.'

I realised that in Laishi I had met a real Christian.

A few days later and I was on a plane back to London. I began thinking about that experience and soon found myself trying to work out the

---

Top Tips for the Upwardly Mobile
boycott companies with poor ethical records (find out via www.ethicalconsumer.org)

best way of relating it to people when I was speaking and preaching. Suddenly I felt very convicted; I was turning it into a story to tell rather than let it really affect me. You see it's hard; I don't live in a slum in Bombay and, as far as I know, no one in my road is dying of AIDS. But there are people in my road who are lonely, who are going through difficult divorces. I do have an elderly neighbour who has no living relatives. There are people in my church who never seem to get invited back to anyone's house for lunch. I suppose we are all like this; all of us are surrounded by people who are left out and who don't fit. People who are socially awkward, bullied or just plain excluded. James says, 'Real religion, the kind that passes muster before God the Father, is this: Reach out to the homeless and loveless in their plight, and guard against corruption from the godless world' (1:27, *The Message*).

So being upwardly mobile is about finding greater intimacy with Jesus and it's about practising true religion. It's about religion that makes the Father happy, about getting to the heart of what Christianity is. Just the thought of Eddie Izzard makes me smile. I like what he says about Christianity, that somehow we've managed to transform it from Jesus's model of 'hang out and be groovy' into the Church's 'mumbling in cold buildings'. It's true; at times we all need reminding of the pure essence of Jesus's life, the basics that changed the world for ever.

Jesus hung out and did the groovy thing with a particular type of person. He headed straight for Nazareth – winner of the Bognor Regis Award for being the butt of too many jokes – and made his home among the poor. For the rest of his life he stayed with the poor, loving, respecting and leading them.

I don't know about you, but when I think about the poor what sometimes comes to mind is a mixed bag of endless questions, half-coherent answers and a big load of confusion. It's tricky, to say the least, and I'm sure it's not just me who's queuing up for a healthy dose of truth and reality. We all need to know more, to feel more and to act more, but how do we make the connection? We need to hook up with the Almighty and sort ourselves out with some divine perspective on the issue. That's what this book hopes to do. As you read it, have some pictures in your mind; not just the one at the beginning of this book (although this sort of poverty is the reality for billions of people in the world today), but also try to keep in mind some other people too. Try to think of the person at your youth group or church who never gets invited out. Try to think of the person at work, school or college who gets bullied. Know that Jesus came for them.

Top Tips for the Upwardly Mobile
if you are 14 plus, join DV8, the network for young people who want to live out God's heart for the poor (to find out more, ring Tearfund on 0845 355 8355)

1

God's Plan for Revival

Cast your mind back over the last few times that you've been in a church meeting and see if you can remember the word 'revival' being mentioned. The chances are that you've probably come up with a few hits, as the 'R' word has been a bit of a favourite for us in the Church of late. We talk about it, pray about it, some of us even wear the T-shirt. Like the new Beetle or an ageing Elvis, reports and rumours of sightings flit about our world with ever-increasing regularity. Unlike the Beetle or the King, though, we're not entirely sure what it looks like; some are convinced that it will come in the form of stadiums filled with repenting people, others believe that it will follow the pattern of past revivals, with dour-faced Scottish preachers turning up the heat in remote towns and villages.

Interaction
- Have a look at Luke 12:48. What sort of things do you think you've been given? How can you give?
- Have a look at that practical nugget found in Deuteronomy 15. How does God use the idea of a sabbatical year for both ecological and humanitarian good?

I had the privilege of visiting a place that had been through a revival. It had gone through a huge one in the middle years of the twentieth century, and even made it into the revival history books as the East African Revival. At the time, as many as 80 per cent of the people were in Bible-believing churches, enjoying a vibrant relationship with Jesus. Can you imagine how that would look for us today? Transport networks overloaded on Sundays as 45 million people rush to church. Voices of compassion would no longer be the minority, but instead would form a huge majority. Imagine the change it would have on a society, stretching out to the generations to come. Surely there would be no looking back from a time like that?

When we think of Rwanda today, what first comes to mind is not the East African Revival that took place there in the fifties, but the genocide that took place in 1994. Over 1.5 million people were murdered in the fighting between the two tribes of the Hutus and the Tutsis. Millions were raped and many more fled to enormous refugee camps in Burundi and what is now known as Congo. What went wrong? How could something so good, so *God*, become something so evil?

I met a bishop when I was out there. A Hutu, he was a good man, having given shelter to Tutsi people in his diocese during the conflict. Unlike many others in his profession he had stayed with his people, ending up in a refugee camp. Instead of using his cash and connections to flee to the West, this man had remained in serious danger, putting himself at even greater risk by choosing to protect the enemy.

As our conversation progressed, the bishop became less coherent. The troubles had exacted a heavy price, and his ramblings and mumblings became increasingly difficult to understand. Eventually he paused. 'We've just got it wrong,' he said after a while. 'We thought we had it right; we thought we had revival. We taught people that if they believed in Jesus then they would go to heaven and that was it. We never taught them about racism, about loving your neighbour, about the violence in your heart. And when he came to test us, the Devil found enough hatred in us to cause this awful war.'

He was a broken man and, as I listened to him, I found myself feeling surprised and slightly

---

Top Tips for the Upwardly Mobile
join Amnesty International's Urgent Action scheme fast

scornful. After all, I thought, how could you teach the gospel without picking up on issues like racism and personal sin? Before I got too high up on my horse though, something struck me: I wonder what I'm missing. I wonder what blind spots my Christian education in England has produced. If the Devil came and really tested us in the UK, what useful raw materials would he find to set something up?

So we know that God's heart is well pumped for revival but, as the bishop showed, some of our ideas of what it is actually about are a bit simplistic. It's not just about big festivals, full churches and highly charged meetings; it's about something much harder to manufacture. And what might that be? I am convinced that in reality revival is about a real change in people's hearts.

If you fancy some evidence that backs up this claim, there's bags of the stuff in the book of Isaiah. It starts out in the life of an individual and ends up affecting a whole nation. Isaiah 58 is the central passage in the transformation. God brings about his values in society – the staple diet of any definition of revival – and the chapter expresses it perfectly. It forms a sandwich, with the introduction of some people at one end, a platter of promises at the other end and a meaty middle section of instructions detailing how these people can get to those final promises. This is God's plan for revival.

> Shout it aloud, do not hold back. Raise your voice like a trumpet. Declare to my people their rebellion and to the house of Jacob their sins. (58:1)

Having been told to tell off a bunch of people, Isaiah then gets the low-down on exactly where they've been going wrong:

> For day after day they seek me out; they seem eager to know my ways, as if they were a nation that does what is right and has not forsaken the commands of its God. They ask me for just decisions and seem eager for God to come near them. 'Why have we fasted,' they say, 'and you have not seen it? Why have we humbled ourselves, and you have not noticed?' (58:2–3)

Not exactly homicide, is it? If you ask me they don't seem all that different from you and me: keen yet flawed. They knew the rules, the banter and, most of all, how to put on a good show. They were religious, and God had a problem with them; they had a blind spot.

Yet despite their frustration with God, within a few verses God has moved from condemnation to the delivery of some wonderful promises. He vows that their quality of life is about to be dramatically improved:

> Then your light will break forth like the dawn, and your healing will quickly appear; then your righteousness will go before you, and the glory of the Lord will be your rear guard. Then you will call, and the Lord will answer; you will cry for help, and he will say: Here am I. . . . your light will rise in the darkness, and your night will become like the noonday. The Lord will guide you

---

always; he will satisfy your needs in a sun-
scorched land and will strengthen your
frame. You will be like a well-watered garden,
like a spring whose waters never fail.
(58:8–11)

Not only does God promise to have a profound
impact on their lives, he also assures them that
they will in turn have a profound impact on the
lives of the people around them. These verses
promising the advancement of God's kingdom
are, to my mind, as clear as any definition of
revival that we could hope to find. After all, if
God had promised to guide you always and
satisfy all your needs, you wouldn't exactly be
miffed now, would you?

Before we get too carried away with the history
lesson, I'm convinced that what God said to his
people through his prophet Isaiah can be equally
applied to us. You see, doing well as a Christian
is not all about reciting the rules or having a
wonderfully executed feasting timetable. It's
about getting closer to God – allowing him to
bless us – and then responding to his call to go
out and take it to everybody else. In the middle

of chapter 58 is a section dealing with all the issues that the Israelites had to get sorted out; in highlighting these issues, God is giving them a direct reply to their question about why he is

---

Problems and Solutions

There's a strange paradox at work in the heart of my faith: the longer I've been a Christian, the less sense things seem to make. Nothing makes sense quite like it used to. When I was short of height and scabby of knee everything seemed clear. If I was a good little chap, said my prayers nightly and tried not to lie and steal, everything would be as sweet as the proverbial nut. These days it's all a little different. I'm still trying to make sure I say my prayers and all the rest, but it just doesn't seem to be enough.

Of course it's right that I feel this way – after all, Jesus didn't simply offer membership for a social club, one that exists just to keep us from getting bored when Sunday TV's looking dull. Yes, it's right that we all find out more about how our faith should affect the whole of our lives, but there's more to my confusion than that.

not hearing their prayers and why he has not sparked revival.

> Your fasting ends in quarrelling and strife, and in striking each other with wicked fists. You cannot fast as you do today and expect your voice to be heard on high. Is this the kind of fast I have chosen, only a day for a man to humble himself? Is it only for bowing one's head like a reed and for lying on sackcloth and ashes? It that what you call a fast, a day acceptable to the Lord?
>
> Is not this the kind of fasting I have chosen: to loose the chains of injustice and untie the cords of the yoke, to set the oppressed free and break every yoke? Is it not to share your food with the hungry and to provide the poor wanderer with shelter – when you see the naked, to clothe him, and not to turn away from your own flesh and blood? (58:4–7)

You see what it's about? It's not just about the prayer and the fasting, the worship and the feasts. Of course those are key ingredients, but that's

---

Top Tips for the Upwardly Mobile
give away more than you spend on yourself

just it; they are part of many other vital components in the kingdom of God. Without the rest – the longing for justice, compassion and action – God's people were left with an unfulfilled desire for something more. Sound familiar?

Martin Luther said that an empty stomach has no ears to hear. Unfortunately many of us today believe that the answer to a hungry child, a homeless man or a dying mother is to hear about Jesus. Worse still, we take this to its most literal extreme, relying purely on words to let them know about God's Son. Instead – like Isaiah's audience – we need to learn how to provide the practical solution to the practical problem. We need to feed the hungry, home the homeless, befriend the outcast. Do these sound like second best? Of course they're not; these are precisely the things on God's agenda that come screaming at us from the pages of the Bible.

Before you get too far with ideas of how you can outsource your social action work, subcontracting the dirty stuff to the people in the church who 'have a heart' for the soup run, think again. The early church didn't compartmentalise their faith; instead they managed to find the knack of integrating it into the whole of their lives. Acts 2:42–7 – immediately after that huge Spirit-fest known as Pentecost – lets us peep through the curtain at the church's private life:

> They devoted themselves to the apostles' teaching and to the fellowship, to the breaking of bread and to prayer. Everyone was filled with awe, and many wonders and miraculous signs were done by the apostles. All the believers were together and had everything in common. Selling their possessions and goods, they gave to anyone as he had need. Every day they continued to meet together in the temple courts. They broke bread in their homes and ate together with glad and sincere hearts, praising God and enjoying the favour of all the people. And the Lord added to their number daily those who were being saved.

You get that bit about how the Lord 'added to their number daily'? Such a phenomenal growth was due to their integration of all aspects of God's character: prayer and action, worship and sacrifice. They sold their stuff, lived together and signed up for a truly radical life. And God, it would seem, was chuffed.

Skip forward to Acts 15 where we see Paul and Barnabas about to go on the most trouser-browning of trouser-browning meetings. They go to Jerusalem to discuss a massive change in Christianity; instead of keeping it for themselves, Paul wants to take the good news out beyond the Jews to the Gentiles. Referring back to it in his letter to the Galatians (chapter 2) Paul's main concern seems to be to continue to remember the poor. Imagine that: he's about to change the face of Christianity for ever, and the main emphasis is still to be remembering the poor.

There's even more evidence in John's first letter:

This is how we know what love is: Jesus Christ laid down his life for us. And we ought to lay down our lives for our brothers.

Top Tips for the Upwardly Mobile
hang out with the person whom people find awkward

> If anyone has material possessions and sees
> his brother in need but has no pity on him,
> how can the love of God be in him? Dear
> children, let us not love with words or
> tongue but with actions and in truth. (3:16–
> 18)

The gospel that we have is a practical one. When
it came to sorting the people out through his
man Isaiah, God sent a strong message that they
had missed the point. They had the 'spiritual'
side of things sorted, but there was a whole other
side that they had ignored. Doing it, meeting
people, living sacrificial lives that others might
have better ones themselves . . . you name it,
they'd forgotten it.

I was once involved with a university Christian
Union's mission week. They told me how they
wanted to do things a little differently to how
they had been done previously, and decided that
instead of the usual band and evangelist gigs they
were going to focus on social justice. They got a
whole load of material together on various
projects, ran a café and got as many people as
possible involved in raising awareness, cash and

generally campaigning for those around the world who hadn't had the same breaks as themselves. You know what happened? They had more people become Christians in that one year than they had in the previous three years' missions put together. It was pure Isaiah 58. Nice.

So what's this Isaiah 58 stuff all about then? Well, there are some really simple things in it: don't hit each other, don't go back on the promises that you make to God, share your food, get freedom for the oppressed, provide what people need. It says that we should treat workers properly. 'Aha!' you may say. 'But I don't employ anyone.' Don't you? I wonder who made those trainers or that jacket of yours. Were they paid a fair wage and given good working conditions, or were they exploited and their lives put in danger?

Top Tips for the Upwardly Mobile
encourage your friends to join you

2

God's Heart for the Poor

So just who are the poor? I mean, it's so easy, isn't it, to convince yourself that the poor are separate from us; on another continent, in a different time? Those barriers of language and culture serve ever so neatly to keep them apart from us, to keep them away from the vulnerability of our ever believing that we could help them. Among some of us rich Christians here in the West there is even the bizarre notion that suffering the ravages of famine and poverty is all part of the way of life for people in the Third World, as if 'it's in their culture, innit?' Unfortunately for us rich Christians in the West, God doesn't quite see it that way.

You see, God likes the poor – and I don't mean because he has to. In fact, God's thing for the poor goes beyond tossing a quid on to the crumpled cardboard of a street-sleeper's pillow; it goes all the way to the core of his being. God's heart beats and breaks for those that have less, for those who are in the wrong place at the wrong time with the wrong passport and the wrong face. He is fair beyond our most liberal descriptions of fairness, generous beyond our wildest dreams and extreme beyond our most vivid nightmares.

Before I get too carried away let's do some study and see exactly who the Bible says these people are that we call 'poor'. In the Hebrew, the Old Testament uses a few words for the poor: *anaw, ani, dal, ebyon* and *ras*. Between them they define some fairly specific circumstances, like someone who is wrongfully impoverished or dispossessed, a beggar imploring charity or a thin, weak, deprived peasant. By the time we get to the New Testament, the main word used for the poor is *ptochos*, meaning someone who is completely destitute and must take help from others. *Ptochos* is the Greek equivalent of *ani* or *dal*, so that means that we can say that the main definition of the poor throughout Scripture relates to being of low economic status, usually due to disaster or some form of oppression.

God has made a point of sticking with this most 'unappealing' bunch of people throughout history. Through Moses he broke the Israelites out of a horrific form of oppression at the hands of the Egyptians, and when Jesus turned up, he did so quoting Isaiah 58 and laying it all on the line in favour of the poor. Turn to the book of Deuteronomy and you're greeted by the policy details surrounding the setting up of the Promised Land. Guess what, God wants it to be a place where 'there should be no poor among you' (15:4). According to the Almighty, there's more than enough to go round, so no one need miss out. Does that remind you of anything? (Hint: even today there is more than enough food in the world to make sure that every person is fed their daily requirement for a healthy diet.)

Or there's the book of Isaiah. We've already stumbled across some of its dynamite in the fifty-eighth chapter, but there's plenty more where that came from. Chapter 3 contains a wild polemic against those who have profited by exploiting and 'crushing the faces of the poor' (v. 15). Through the prophet Isaiah God goes on to give specific details of what he has found offensive.

> The women of Zion are haughty, walking along with outstretched necks, flirting with their eyes, tripping along with mincing steps, with ornaments on their ankles . . .

However, it's not just about posture or deportment; God goes in for the kill by listing the purchases that have been made with money plundered from the poor. Alongside bangles, headbands, crescent necklaces, earrings, bracelets and veils are headdresses, ankle chains, sashes, perfume, charms, rings, clothes, purses, mirrors, linen garments, tiaras and shawls. What about you? What are the 'must have' purchases that catch both your eye and your wallet? What do you justify in the name of fashion?

For the guys and girls of Zion, fashion had become a serious business; so serious in fact that they were willing to do whatever was necessary to make sure that they had the Next Best Thing before it became So *Last Week*, Darling. The trouble was that 'whatever was necessary' often turned out to be dumping on the poor by making them work harder for less. I wonder if that sounds familiar too . . .

But why the poor? Why didn't God side with the beautiful people instead? After all, aren't the wealthy so much more *attractive*, so much more *desirable*? I can just imagine the conversation between some exquisitely labelled PR chick giving a sales pitch to the returning Son of God:

'OK darling, so let's talk about the face of the campaign. I'm thinking Jodie or Amber. Be a sweetie and get me another Café Latte, would you?'

'I was actually thinking about the streets.'

'Mmmmm, yes, Urban Angst; love it, darling. I can see it now; Heroin Chic in a Muji bedsit.'

'Someone from Sierra Leone . . .'

'You want to discover someone, do you? Well I'm not so sure myself . . .'

'He lost an arm when he was four and contracted glaucoma when he was eight. His legs are crippled from early malnutrition and his family are dead.'

Pause. 'Would Johnny Depp be any good?'

God sides with the poor because they are closest to his heart. After all, 'He who mocks the poor shows contempt for their Maker' (Proverbs 17:5). There's no denying the fact, uncomfortable as it may seem, that Jesus made sure that they were right at the top of his agenda.

Top Tips for the Upwardly Mobile
ring Tearfund on 0845 355 8355 and ask for Activist, a magazine which aims to inform young people of global concerns and give you opportunities for action

It was a message that he successfully managed to pass on to his disciples and followers too, as the New Testament clearly shows. In my opinion, one of the best examples of this is James's letter to the believers that had been scattered among the nations. He was interested in what it meant to be a Christian, in finding out precisely what defined authentic Christianity. After all, it's fine to say that you believe it, but living it out for all to see in glorious Technicolor® is surely the ultimate test of whether our faith is real. Throughout his book, James gets down to the nitty-gritty of dealing with some hard issues: coping when things are going disastrously wrong, handling persecution, exploring the differences that exist between rich and poor, between learning about things and actually doing them, between talking about following Jesus and actually submitting to and being changed by him. He is ultra keen to point out just how much of a heart God has for the poor, as well as to paint a few pictures that describe a little of what this new community of believers should look like. He explains what that means for rich people as well as for poor people, suggesting that 'The brother in humble circumstances ought to take pride in his high position' (James 1:9). In other words, we all ought to be going against society's flow; instead of thinking of himself as the world does, the poor man ought to be aware and proud of his high standing. Instead of being second rate and despised, the poor man is just as much in line for the inheritance of the kingdom of heaven as the man with a swollen wallet. The rich, on the other hand, should take pride in their low position; once their life is up what follows will be a swift, possession-free exit from this life into the next.

There's even more spiritual and social dynamite when we get to chapter 2. There, in the second verse, James talks about favouritism, drawing our attention to the variations in our reactions to people depending on whether we consider them to be rich, powerful, poor or weak. There's nothing quite as frustrating as chatting to someone when you notice that they're not looking at your shoulder to check for dandruff or slipped pads, but they're actually looking past said shoulder and at another, more important, person in the vicinity.

James works out a scenario just like this:

Suppose a man comes into your meeting wearing a gold ring and fine clothes, and a poor man in shabby clothes also comes in. If you show special attention to the man

---

Problems and Solutions

People like me, writing books like this for people like you, often chuck out batch after batch of statistics to support their case. Rightly so, for there is something shocking about perceiving the scale of injustice; something about all those billions that acts as a cold shower to our warm and toasty attitudes of self-preservation. Try these on for size:

- People in Europe spend more on ice-cream each year than it would cost to provide clean water and sanitation for all people in developing countries (United Nations Development Programme (UNDP), *Human Development Report* (HDR) Overview, 1998, p. 37)
- A child born in the industrial world adds more to consumption and pollution over

---

his or her lifetime than more than 30 children born in developing countries (HDR Overview, 1998, p. 1)

- More than 100 million people in rich nations are homeless; over 37 million are without jobs (HDR Overview, 1998, p. 6)
- Aid to the poorest countries is at its lowest level in ten years. World aid fell from £37 billion in 1996 to £32 billion in 1998 (Judith Randel and Tony German, *The Reality of Aid*, 1998/9)
- Some 300,000 children around the world are fighting wars (UNICEF, *The State of the World's Children*, 1999)

Ice-cream ... 30 times more consumption ... 100 million homeless ... aid falling by £5 billion ... 300,000 children fighting wars. Yes, these figures and facts are shocking, but there's something else about them that's worth mentioning: it's all too easy for us to think of them as figures, *just* figures. These faceless millions, the ones we've all heard about and seen before can all too easily become part of the furniture: far from ideal but too much hassle to correct. But stop just one minute. Read Matthew 25:31–

46 and think about it carefully. Instead of nameless faces, statistics without meaning, Jesus points to real people. When did you last see Jesus hungry, thirsty, a stranger, naked, sick or in prison?

wearing fine clothes and say, 'Here's a good seat for you,' but say to the poor man, 'You stand there' or 'Sit on the floor by my feet,' have you not discriminated among yourselves and become judges with evil thoughts? (2:2–4)

And he goes on to say:

Has not God chosen those who are poor in the eyes of the world to be rich in faith and to inherit the kingdom he promised those who love him? But you have insulted the poor. (2:5–6)

As well as being hugely dramatic, these verses are of vital importance to us. Not only is James

---

Top Tips for the Upwardly Mobile
look beyond the headlines to the truth that lies behind

telling us to be nice to other people, he is also encouraging us to check the state of our own heart when it comes to the formation of our first impressions and the actions that follow. He tells us to be honest with ourselves. Do we warm to the beautiful person and withdraw at the sight of someone ugly? Do we turn towards the wealthy like a flower towards the sun and do we turn away from the poor with equal speed and determination, fearful that poverty may be contagious? But James goes even further; it is precisely the people who have nothing, the ones who are dependent on God whom God has promised his kingdom to. These are the people that we need to honour, to respect and treat as our betters.

Interaction

- There is no shortage of poor people around today. The United Nations Development Programme's *Human Development Report* in 1998 suggests that of the 4.4 billion people in developing countries, nearly three-fifths lack basic sanitation. Almost a third have no access to clean water. A quarter do not have adequate housing. A fifth of children have left school by the time they reach double figures and a fifth have no access to modern health services. About a fifth do not have enough dietary energy and protein. Other deficiencies are even more common; for example, worldwide, 2 billion people are anaemic, including 55 million in industrial countries.

- The gap between the largest and the smallest consumers is vast. Globally, the richest 20 per cent of the world's people account for 86 per cent of total private consumption expenditures – the poorest 20 per cent a minuscule 1.3 per cent. More specifically, the richest fifth:
  - consume 45 per cent of all meat and fish, the poorest fifth 5 per cent
  - consume 58 per cent of total energy, the poorest fifth less than 4 per cent
  - have 74 per cent of all telephone lines, the poorest fifth 1.5 per cent
  - consume 84 per cent of all paper, the poorest fifth 1.1 per cent
  - own 87 per cent of the world's vehicle fleet, the poorest fifth less than 1 per cent.

Later on in the chapter James goes even further. There's a hot debate raging about just what it is that makes a Christian. Many are holding up their beliefs like Boy Scout badges, waving them and declaring 'Well I *must* be a Christian; look, I've got *Healing*'. 'Ah,' comes the reply. 'Well I've got *Spiritual Warfare*.'

Enter James, stage left:

> What good is it, my brothers, if a man claims to have faith but has no deeds? Can such faith save him? Suppose a brother or sister is without clothes and daily food. If one of you says to him, 'Go, I wish you well; keep warm and well fed,' but does nothing about his physical needs, what good is it? (2:14–16)

He has hit on a profound truth here; prayer is good, but rates a zero on the nutritional scale. You cannot eat, drink or be intravenously fed prayer. Therefore if someone is hungry, what good does it do to say, 'Aah, bless. I'll say a prayer for you'? They need food. Simple as that.

Top Tips for the Upwardly Mobile
use your vote

> In the same way, faith by itself, if it is not accompanied by action, is dead. But someone will say, 'You have faith; I have deeds.' Show me your faith without deeds, and I will show you my faith by what I do. (2:17–18)

This is the key to James's argument; it's no use just singing the songs and preaching the message from the pulpit – God is interested in what we do, not simply in whether we believe in him; after all 'even the demons believe that' (v. 19). In other words, just believing the stuff doesn't actually count for a whole lot in itself, although it does put you on the same ranking as a demon. Which is nice.

To be absolutely clear about it all, James spells it out in verse 20:

> You foolish man, do you want evidence that faith without deeds is useless?

Finally, the book closes with the writer addressing himself to the rich.

> Now listen, you rich people, weep and wail
> because of the misery that is coming upon
> you. (5:1)

We've all seen the National Lottery show where they let the cameras in on the lives of previous jackpot winners. It's smiles all round and the message that screams across the subconscious waveband is 'This is Success – don't you want to be like them?' James, on the other hand, sees it differently, as by the time judgment day comes along all that glitters will count for nothing. Even worse, there will be a serious lack of value attached to such goods. By then

> Your wealth has rotted, and moths have
> eaten your clothes. Your gold and silver are
> corroded. Their corrosion will testify against
> you and eat your flesh like fire. You have
> hoarded wealth in the last days. (5:2–3)

Instead of guaranteeing an automatic entry on the guest-list through the Pearly Gates, all that *stuff* will actually count against the rich. To put it mildly, it will be a bit of an embarrassment –

and that won't be because the angels will be saying, 'Oh no darling, Gucci is *so* passé.'

He goes on:

> The wages you failed to pay the workmen who mowed your fields are crying out against you. The cries of the harvesters have reached the ears of the Lord Almighty. (5:4)

When we get cheap bargains because Third World workers have been poorly paid and forced to work in unsafe conditions, that cries out against us and reaches the ears of God himself. He doesn't compliment us on the bargain purchase; instead he rails against the injustice.

> You have lived on earth in luxury and self-indulgence. You have fattened yourselves in the day of slaughter. (5:5)

A bit over the top, perhaps? Maybe we can brush it aside as only being relevant to a culture that existed a couple of millennia back. Unfortunately, we'd be wrong to assume that. The day of slaughter is here, now. There are people dying of malnutrition, people dying of easily preventable illnesses. We in the West consume more than our fair share of protein, meat, energy and other resources. We fatten ourselves for the day of slaughter.

I was on a trip to India with Tearfund once, visiting people we work with in Bombay. I had a day off in the middle and was taken by a friend to a place called the Gate of India, in the city's bay. There's an expensive hotel there called the Taj as well as plenty of street entertainers, snake-charmers, stalls and the like. It's a fun place to be and it's awash with tourists. It's also full of children who are begging. Having got wise to the way of the world, whenever they see a western person they tend to bombard them with requests for cash. My friend advised me not to give them anything as once you started it wouldn't take long before a crowd of forty children might be chasing you. The whole thing could get a little scary and it was best left alone.

Having looked around we got into a taxi and

headed off to our next destination. The cab stopped at some traffic lights right outside the Taj Hotel and, as usual, while we waited people approached the open windows to try and sell us goods or to beg. One girl walked up, put her hand into the taxi, palm up, and looked at me. 'Please, Uncle,' she said. Uncle's a term of respect in India, used in much the same way that we would say 'sir'. I looked at the girl and saw that she was around ten or twelve, was very beautiful and dressed in a piece of cloth. Again she asked for money, 'Please, Uncle.'

The traffic lights changed and we moved on before I had a chance to get any money out. I turned to my friend and said how beautiful she was. 'Yes,' he replied. 'She was, wasn't she? It's a shame, as within a year or two she'll probably be a prostitute and then she'll be lucky to make it into her twenties.'

It was later on that night as I was thinking about my day that I realised I knew who that little girl was. Her name was Jesus. One day I'll stand in front of him and hear the words coming at me: 'I was hungry and you did not feed me. I was thirsty and you did not give me a drink. I was a stranger and you did not invite me in, naked and you did not clothe me.'

And I'll say, 'But when didn't I do these things?'

He'll say, 'You were in a taxi in Bombay, waiting for the traffic lights outside the Taj Hotel to change. For as much as you did not do it for the least of these, my brothers and sisters, you did not do it for me.'

That's a really personal story, perhaps the most personal story I could tell. It's that little girl's face that I think of when I cannot sleep at night, worrying about work. I regularly wonder where she is now, and I know that in her I met Jesus. In Matthew 25 that's exactly what Jesus said. He explained that he is found with the poorest of the poor, that he is found with the ones who have nothing, in the beggar and the orphan, the lonely and the street child, the bullied person and the ones that hurt. He looks at you and me and asks a simple question: will

Top Tips for the Upwardly Mobile
write to your MP

you help me? These are people made in his image: will we bless him? Will we worship him?

Things get scary in Matthew 25 because the only difference between those who went to heaven and those who went to hell is found on the basis of what they did or did not do for precisely these people. Did they feed, clothe, help, spend time with them and offer them shelter? If the answer was yes they went one way, if it was no, they went the other. Read it for yourself; it's frighteningly simple. I've heard people try and twist it, interpreting it this way and that, but in truth the passage cannot be watered down. It stands out, bold and uncompromising, perfectly clear for all to see and understand. Do we serve the poor? No? We cannot call ourselves Christians then.

The truth is that God could have hand-picked a nation of wealthy, successful types, but instead he chose the Israelites. He could have made up a great team of doers and achievers, people with a decent track record and proven management experience, but he chose the apostles. He could have picked a political insider, someone who would have instantly commanded respect, but he chose to come as Jesus. God has gone out of his way not only to help the poor, but to perform his work through them.

These are no isolated acts of wild abandon, no spontaneous and crazy deeds regretted in the cold light of day, but part of a calculated strategy: God's masterplan. Jesus made it clear to all of us that he was turning up the heat when he rewrote the rule book. Instead of the law being mainly a series of sins to avoid, Jesus made it clear that the top two consist of loving God with all our heart, soul and mind as well as loving our neighbour as we love ourselves. This puts love at the heart of the law, and turns our goal into active spreading instead of passive avoiding.

Case Study

Personal story, from Kizito, Uganda:

'I am fourteen years old and both my parents have died. Sister Rachael helped me to start an income-generating activity by giving me two rabbits! When I am able to rear and sell rabbits I get money which helps to pay for my school fees and books. I want to have a big farm and lots of rabbits so that I can pay my own school fees and also look after my brothers and sisters in the future.'

3

God's Idea of Success

Upwardly Mobile, huh? If being mobile in an upwards kind of direction is a pot of gold, I wonder what the rainbow that leads to it looks like? How do we get there, how do we define it? Could it be a glittering career, a waxed and polished BMW and a house with a sweeping driveway? Perhaps that's too much; perhaps we can call ourselves Upwardly Mobile — or successful – simply by being the best: winning the respect of our peers and having enough cash to take that nice holiday each year, run a car and eat out a couple of times each week. Then again, perhaps even that's going too far: could it be that we become successful once we've got just that little bit more than the person down the street? I think not. Want to know what being Upwardly Mobile is really all about? It's about doing things God's way, and, unfortunately for some, God's not impressed by the shine on our car, the thickness of our wad of cash or the comfort of our lifestyle.

We all know the glow of pride that results from a nice dose of public affirmation. It may have been the awarding of a gold star back in primary school for our outstanding contribution to the sandpit, or it may have been a pat on the back from our coach for a goal well scored. Chests puffed out with pride, we can thrive on these moments, treasuring them deep inside. But imagine how great it would feel to cop a load of public respect from the Creator of the Universe himself? John the Baptist received just such an affirmation when Jesus said that, among everyone born, there had been no one greater than John. As far as references go, that one's got to carry some serious weight.

John was no stranger to crowds; people flocked to be near him, to hear his teaching and to get baptised by him out in the desert. He pulled huge crowds as the 'voice of one calling in the desert, "Prepare the way for the Lord, make straight paths for him" ' (Luke 3:4). He got the people ready for Jesus, preaching about the need for repentance and encouraging those who were into his message to get baptised as a symbolic gesture that helped to express their desire to change their lives.

As the hottest show in town you might expect that John buttered up his crowds, telling them 'You've been a lovely audience' before signing off with a few well-oiled mother-in-law jokes. Wrong. John opted for the shock tactic, calling his listeners a 'brood of vipers' (Luke 3:7). He went on:

Top Tips for the Upwardly Mobile
ring Tearfund on 0845 355 8355 and get hold of the
World Watch Prayer Link so that you can pray effectively

> Who warned you to flee from the coming
> wrath? Produce fruit that is in keeping with
> repentance. And do not begin to say to
> yourselves, 'We have Abraham as our
> father.' (3:7–8)

In other words, he's giving them a quick slap for
trying to justify their unholy lives by claiming
that their family connections would sort them
out. Merely being an Israelite, a descendant of
Abraham, was not enough to get a tick in God's
Register of Success. Being wise, they asked him
what they had to do to be considered something
better than a viper. John's answer is fascinating.
Here's the guy who is making the way ready for
Jesus, setting the scene by teaching people about
the need to change, while Jesus would come later
and teach people about the kingdom of God, the
way to change.

According to John, the way to change is
simple. If you've got two tunics (it says in verse
11), share with the man who has none. Likewise,
if you've got a well-stocked fridge, share it with
the person who is without. Some tax collectors

asked him what advice he had for them. 'Don't collect any more than you are required to' was the answer. Then came some soldiers keen for a bit of insight into their own specific situations. 'Don't extort money and don't accuse people falsely – be content with your pay', they were told.

These are interesting points. He's talking about repentance, going through the theory that lies behind God's new kingdom. His answers form a blueprint, a map that leads towards God's kingdom, and his three pieces of advice are brilliantly simple. He talks about sharing in a time of plenty, about being honest with money and about not abusing your power. The scene has been set.

When I was in India I spent time with some of the poorest people I've ever met. Sitting in their home, wearing clothes that would have cost more than they had to live on for an entire year, I was blown away by their outrageous generosity. They were living in the middle of the poorest slum, opening up their doors to the lowest and most despised of their neighbours. The homeless children who were living with Aids had nowhere to go, but this couple provided them with schooling and somewhere to stay. I have never been so struck by the presence of Jesus.

There's another couple I know, possibly one of the richest. They have a beautiful house in a beautiful village. There's nothing that they need, and they could afford most of the things they want. But they make me think about God too. Their income is way higher than their lifestyle, and through them hundreds of people have been helped, either with money, accommodation, support or time. You name it, and they probably give it.

These couples have something in common. They both give until it hurts, and then some more. They both make sacrifices, going without for the sake of someone else's gain. Both couples focus on God, asking him what he wants them to do. They both obey the call. They both remind me of God's idea of success.

Sunday schools tend to feed children a

Top Tips for the Upwardly Mobile
join a bank that does not lend to impoverished countries

reasonably standard menu of spiritual lessons. Instead of sermons there are stories, and instead of personal illustrations from the speaker's life, the characters in the Bible are brought to life in front of the student's eyes. There are some absolutely classic biblical stories that get covered: Noah and the ark, Daniel in the lions' den, David and Goliath, as well as the one about that bloke who got swallowed by an overgrown trout. There are plenty more diamonds I could mention, and even if you've had no history of sitting cross-legged in Sunday school sessions, the chances are that you'll have heard of the story of Zacchaeus. 'Zacchaeus was a little man' we used to sing when I was cross-legged on the carpet at St James, Croxley Green. Funny that, because at the time so was I, and I didn't notice anyone rushing to make up a song about me. I even liked climbing trees!

Anyway, the whole thing about Zacchaeus is that he was a blagger. He was wide, 'aving it large and generally doing a bit of a Robin Hood on all his good neighbours in the hood. The only difference between this Jewish Robin Hood and

our green-tighted one from Nottingham was that
Zac managed to steal not only from the rich, but
the poor too. Oh, and he never gave any away,
either.

So Zacchaeus was working his scams all over
the place, collecting taxes from the local Jews and
– after taking a cut for his own considerable
expenses incurred along the way – paying said
taxes to the Romans. Apparently he didn't have a
straight bone in his body, and over the years he
had become a dab hand at greasing the palms of
those in a position of influence above him, as
well as at encouraging the introduction of Roman
heavies into the 'negotiation' process, should a
Jewish taxpayer refuse to cough up whatever
ludicrous sum our little friend had mentioned.
He didn't seem to care that his greed caused
people to go hungry or that it turned others out
on to the streets. He was unfair and unjust, but
none of that mattered as long as he looked after
number one.

Needless to say, Zacchaeus was not universally
loved. Walking down the street did not require
him to negotiate skilfully the obstacles of bodies

prostrated on the ground in praise of his most noble character. So when Jesus singled him out as the chosen one in the town with whom he would hang out for a few hours, there was more than a gentle murmur of confusion among the crowd.

Problems and Solutions
Dream big, we are told. Whatever you are going to do, do it large. Don't just settle for life in the slow lane, take control and raise the revs of your spiritual activity. Launch a new project. Set up a skate park. Storm the media.

The trouble is that in the back of my mind is a nagging little thought that won't go away. Sure, I'm 100 per cent up for believing that Christianity has the power to change the face of the world, but it's just this question of 'how' that bugs me. I wonder if all this talk of 'doing it large', all this *size matters* stuff might be taking us away from the point.

It's all too easy to stand at the sidelines and come up with the conclusion that Christianity is best carried out by the good-looking people on the stage. Those confident people seem to be so well connected, so able to produce results, so 'blessed' with the Midas touch that anything we might attempt will only end up just a pale reflection.

And this is where the problems come: it's all too easy to stand at the side and think, 'Well, that could never be me, so I'd best leave it to the talented ones.' We make our excuses and back out from the prospect of ever really *doing* anything. After all, we tell ourselves, they seem to be able to do it so much better, to get so much more applause and *wow*, that our contribution is bound to be worthless. Nice excuse, but I'm afraid that it just won't wash. There's nothing in the Bible that says that Christianity is only for the high achievers. Christianity is for all, not only because it is open to everyone but because it can relate to anyone. Through his teaching – and particularly through the sermon on the mount – Jesus offered a fresh way to look at and act in the world. He didn't give advice on how to stage the best events: he taught how to live out a life. Attitude, reaction, ambition and judgment: all areas in which we can follow his lead.

Sure, the big gigs are good too, but let's not forget that we can all make a difference. It might be quieter, we might never receive much in the way of recognition, but do we really believe that we're supposed to be signing up for Carnival Christianity, the sort where the most eye-catching stuff wins?

Yet Jesus chose him nevertheless. Perhaps there may have been people in the crowd who had done even worse things than crooked old Zacchaeus – we can say for sure that there were plenty of people who had managed to live better lives than the tax collector and were therefore much more 'deserving' of Jesus's time. But Jesus made a hugely potent point. He singled out the corruption and injustice of one man in order to send a message throughout the rest of time: it's not right and it's not OK. Trampling on the lives of others in order to advance your own wallet is not on, and following Jesus means taking a stand against it.

So what, you may be wondering, went on in Zacchaeus's house? Did Jesus do a spiritual Bruce Lee on him and beat all that evil pus from out of his system? I think not. Here's the story from the top:

Jesus entered Jericho and was passing through. A man was there by the name of Zacchaeus; he was a chief tax collector and was wealthy. He wanted to see who Jesus was, but being a short man he could not, because of the crowd. So he ran ahead and climbed a sycamore-fig tree to see him, since Jesus was coming that way. When Jesus reached the spot, he looked up and said to him, 'Zacchaeus, come down immediately. I must stay at your house today.' So he came down at once and welcomed him gladly. All the people saw this and began to mutter, 'He has gone to be the guest of a "sinner." ' But Zacchaeus stood up and said to the Lord, 'Look, Lord! Here and now I give half of my possessions to the poor, and if I have cheated anybody out of anything, I will pay back four times the amount.' Jesus said to him, 'Today salvation has come to this house, because this man, too, is a son of Abraham. For the Son of Man came to seek and to save what was lost.' (Luke 19:1–10)

It's a little unclear as to when Zacchaeus had his massive change of heart, but I think it's safe to assume that there was a gap between him and Jesus heading off chez Zac and his public declaration of honesty and integrity. What happened was simply that the Son of God invited the sinner to spend time with him. Contrary to popular opinion, God doesn't melt when confronted by the ugliness of sin (just check out the number of times Jesus opted for the company of prostitutes, money men and the unclean instead of the religious elite). In fact, it's far more likely that the exact opposite will happen; it is the sinner who will find themselves overpowered by the loving acceptance of the Almighty. This is what happened with our man Zac; he spent time with Jesus – surrounded as he was in his own home by the spoils of his misspent life – accepted his offer of friendship and turned towards him.

But there's more. Zacchaeus didn't just come out with his hands up, waving a white flag and admitting his guilt. He didn't just say 'fair cop' and hand the money back. Instead he left his one-on-one with God's son an utterly changed man. He was prepared to pay back all those he had screwed by four times the amount. I may never have been that great at maths, but I'm sure that if you pay out four times what you have received, you'll probably end up bankrupt. And so we witness the full transformation of the tax collector; he goes from fraudster to someone who gives at great personal cost. And so Jesus takes out his highlighter pen and draws a fat luminous pink line underneath the message: this is what it's all about; giving rather than keeping, honouring the poor, pointing the way to the time when the first really will be last and the last really will be first.

Interaction

- Think about your own spiritual ambitions. Are they tied in with getting recognition from your peers? Can you imagine doing stuff that nobody will notice?

- If *Hello* magazine was to make a list of the country's ten most successful people, who do you think would be on it? Once you've made your list, compare it with others and see whether there is any difference between definitions of success.
- If God's idea of success boils down to obedience, sacrifice and relationship with him, who are some of the most successful people that you know?
- Examine Isaiah 1:10–15, 58:3–7 and Amos 5:21–4, Matthew 25:41–3. Talk about how these passages make you feel – perhaps a little daunted or maybe determined. How fundamental are these verses to your view of God? Do they change the way you see him? How will you feel about them tomorrow?

God works through acts that carry something of his image – for example justice, compassion and love – and as Christians we don't have the monopoly on good works. But it is important to note that God works particularly through those who are 'being transformed into his [Jesus's] likeness' (2 Corinthians 3:18), people who are able to sign up for the whole package.

While we're on the subject of Sunday school classics, there are a few more that are well worth a mention. One of the most famous stories in the Bible – and an absolutely key story for any Sunday school – is of Jesus feeding the five thousand. We all know it: Jesus had been holding a conference, teaching the crowds about the kingdom of God and chucking in a bit of healing for good measure. It had been going on all day and as evening approached the disciples raised the point of food. Jesus said something typically dramatic, suggesting that the disciples give them something to eat.

Usually when telling this story we fast forward to the bit with the five loaves and two fish, the bottomless baskets, general munching and total satisfaction. Unfortunately this misses out some of the most dramatic aspects of the whole passage. You see, two supremely radical things happened here. First up, we need to get it clear

---

Top Tips for the Upwardly Mobile
try living for a few days on the typical daily food ration available in a refugee camp

that Jesus, who had been teaching people spiritual truths and healing their bodies, shows that he is as interested in their physical wellbeing as he is in their spiritual wellbeing. Not only is he interested in teaching about the kingdom of God, not only is he up for doing a few miracles, but he is also interested in something as mundane as whether people are hungry.

The next radical thing about the story is that Jesus turns to his disciples – the Church – and says, '*You* feed them'. Providing food was not put down as a job for someone else, perhaps for some underling or trainee disciple; it was their job, their ministry. They had helped him to preach the kingdom as well as to heal the sick, now it was their turn to feed the hungry. So we get a clear picture that feeding people who are hungry is actually kingdom work.

Not surprisingly the disciples' response was similar to ours when we feel the sting of poverty around us; they went for the old 'the need is so great and we have so little' line. How many times have we opted for the same? How often have our lips produced the words 'it's just a drop in the ocean . . . what good will my fiver/time/smile do when there's so much more that needs to be done?' It's true, in terms of pure physics, the little we have doesn't look like it will go far enough. But we miss the point. Jesus wasn't interested in how much they had, just whether he had access to all of it. He didn't need them to have enough to answer the whole problem, he just needed everything they had. Once he had it all in his own hands, it was enough to solve the whole problem.

All across the world there are people making a huge difference in their communities and environments, but who have very little to offer. The key is that they are giving it all. The job of making it meet the need is best left to God.

You can probably tell that I'm about to move on to look at Mother Teresa. She was a true international celebrity and the irony of her death being eclipsed by the shock that surrounded Princess Diana's, just a few days earlier, was not lost on many. Mother Teresa owned nothing apart from a shawl and a bowl out of which she ate and yet the whole world knew her name and what she stood for. Of course, a little old nun living in Calcutta could never achieve an awful lot, but in Jesus's hands her actions were enough to challenge the whole world.

There's another Bible story that we could do with having a quick butcher's at. It's another Sunday school favourite called the widow's offering and we find it in Luke 21. Jesus was at the temple, looking at the various people as they made their way forward to put their gifts in the collection box. He saw the rich people putting their gifts in, and he also saw an elderly widow putting in a couple of coins that would probably have been the equivalent of those pesky little one pence pieces that always seem to get in the way of the nice, oversized and shiny silver ones. He turned to his disciples and spoke:

> 'I tell you the truth,' he said, 'this poor widow has put in more than all the others. All these people gave their gifts out of their wealth; but she out of her poverty put in all she had to live on.' (21:3–4)

Suddenly we're back in the territory of the feeding of the five thousand: Jesus only needs one packed lunch or a couple of virtually worthless coins, and not – as we may protest – the answer to everything. He saw this woman and perceived that through her offering he had access to everything that she had. She put in what she could not afford, laying herself on the line for God. That's power.

There are a couple of points to take from this story. First it's important not to forget how personal it all is. If you happen to earn stacks of cash then tithing isn't really much of a big deal. There comes a point when a thing called disposable comes into the equation, and as long as that particular amount happens to be more than your tithe, giving away your 10 per cent or whatever isn't going to hurt that much. Even if you don't earn much money, putting in what you don't need, what doesn't matter to you is – unfortunately for us Christians – not that important. It's all quite nice, but it's not really

---

Top Tips for the Upwardly Mobile
if you are a youth leader, join Global Action Network to get loads of help in sharing God's heart for the poor with your young people (ring Tearfund on 0845 355 8355)

God's idea of success. Jesus looks and asks what it is that we are giving him that is personal, what it is that we are sacrificing that we cannot afford to be without.

The second point is that God's economy works on very different principles to our human economy. He doesn't need to have huge resources at his disposal, just access to whatever it is that we have. When there is sacrificial giving – whether of money, time or hospitality – God multiplies that gift out of all proportion, and that's where his power lies.

Many of us are fond of having the odd clear-out, sifting the good stuff from the bad and taking the bin-bagged rejects from our homes down to the charity shop, feeling nice and smug as we do. 'I give to charity,' we may tell ourselves on the way to the shop. 'I support my brothers and sisters who are less fortunate.' True, it is a very good thing to do, but unfortunately I don't think it quite makes it into the category of 'giving'. Chucking away our unwanteds and off-loading it all on to Oxfam is not giving, it's clearing out. Let's not kid ourselves by claiming that we 'do our bit' in this way; it's about as close to biblical giving as line dancing is to ballet. Yes, we do need to have regular clear-outs, but those times are not to be confused with giving; that only starts when it's personal.

One of the other all-time great stories is the parable of the good Samaritan (Luke 10:30–37). We all know how it goes: someone comes to Jesus and asks him what needs to be done in order to inherit eternal life. Jesus says, 'Well, what does it say in the law?' The man comes back with an A+ answer, declaring that the law appears to be condensed into two key elements: love the Lord your God with all your heart, soul, strength and mind and love your neighbour as yourself. 'You're right,' says Jesus, 'so get on with it.' It's simple; all we need to do to get eternal life is to love God with all we have inside us and to treat people with as much love as we have for ourselves. Simple to understand, very hard to do. Which explains why the questioner sticks up his hand one more time to ask, 'Well, er, who exactly is my neighbour then?' Cue story . . . man going to Jerusalem . . . robbed and beaten . . . left for

dead ... priest and Levite pass and blank him
... etc., etc., etc.

I don't think that Jesus was using this story as
an excuse to have a pop at religious people;
instead I think that he was looking for some
dramatic tension and intrigue in the tale. People
who were pillars of society, people who were
successful and had made it in the general public's
eye and who should have been setting others
an example end up behaving like the bad guys.
The bloodied man was just too much of an
inconvenience and those that walked by were too
busy to help. Of course, given alternative
circumstances I'm sure many of them would have
been only too happy to help, but you see, that
was just such bad timing old boy. Must dash.

Jesus hits them with the punchline. We all
know that the Samaritans and the Jews hated
each other with a passion, so much so that when
Jesus uttered the 'S' word some of his audience
would have spat on the ground as a knee-jerk
reaction to so vile a race. Where the priest and
the Levite should have done something, this
outcast, this scum, this hated foreigner put them

all to shame. He puts himself out, pays out his own money and takes charge of the victim's well-being. Jesus says to the man who originally quizzed him about salvation and neighbours, 'Which of these three do you think was the neighbour?' The obvious reply comes back, 'The one who had mercy,' and Jesus tells him he's right and suggests that he go off and do likewise.

This is a fascinating story for us Christians. It is an indirect answer to the question 'How do I inherit eternal life?' The first answer is to follow the law, out of which comes a question about an even more specific aspect of Christlike living. The answer is clear: put yourself out for the person that has nothing, the one who can never pay you back, who isn't just family or a friend but who may even be from a different race or social class. It might even be someone that you don't like. Paying the price ourselves, putting ourselves out to care for and treat these people properly, is a classic definition of

---

Top Tips for the Upwardly Mobile
get sponsored to eat brown rice for a week instead of your main meal

loving our neighbour as ourself.

Elsewhere in the New Testament Jesus pointed out that it's not really that hard to love our friends; after all, even the 'pagans' do that. The hard thing – the Christian thing – is to love our enemies. The parable of the good Samaritan shows someone who saw his enemy in need and who acted kindly towards him at his own cost and inconvenience. According to Jesus, that is intimately tied up with inheriting eternal life.

Equal justice is at the heart of God's idea of success. He is so into it that he made sure it became part of the law (Exodus 23:6) and declared through the prophets that ignoring it was a one-way ticket to destruction (try Amos 5:10–15). Jesus carried on the work throughout his ministry, not only by healing and comforting the poor, but by suggesting that we invite a decent spread of people round to dinner (Luke 14:12–14).

We cannot ignore the need for generosity. It is all summed up in 1 John 3:16 which focuses on the fact that Jesus gave the most valuable thing he had – his life – for us. We are told to follow his lead, and then we are given this:

> If anyone has material possessions and sees his brother in need but has no pity on him, how can the love of God be in him? (3:17)

So giving to the poor is the most direct way of imitating Jesus's generosity. Another way of following in his steps is breaking out of the religious and cultural barriers that we erect around us. Jesus made sure that he gave to people other than Jews (like the Samaritan woman and the Roman centurion), and he talked passionately about the shameful attitudes of those who walked along the road before the good Samaritan. This means that our generosity shouldn't just be directed at those who are similarly 'washed in the blood'. No, Christianity is about giving wherever there is need, regardless of the recipient, and without strings or conditions.

Case Study

Personal story, Kazakhstan

'I was fifteen years old when I started using marijuana. I am now twenty-seven. My life from there went down, down, down until I became completely dependent on narcotics. To be honest I couldn't imagine a sober day. I was full of fears or horrors. Then I heard about Jesus and started to pray 'Either kill me, Lord, or save me from this life.' I started attending a cell group and heard of Teen Challenge. I became the first female student in the new programme and have been here for four years, first as a student and now as a worker. I am free! This is a miracle! I don't know how God could handle my stubborn, demanding, selfish and self-centred personality. I don't know how he could love me and be so patient with me. But all these things he did. I am learning to accept myself and love other people.'

4

God's Next Step

We've already established that Jesus made some
hefty changes to Judaism. Instead of the law
being largely about things that people should
avoid, he introduced the idea that the main
agenda was getting on with the job of loving God
and loving others. In case you're wondering, that's
not a cue for serial flirting, but for expressing
God's generous, sacrificial heart for the poor.

In the same way as he rewrote the rules for success, Jesus also gave a few tweaks to traditional ideas of failure. Suddenly life was about relationship, about getting closer to God. We still have things in common with the ancients though: they shared our struggle to keep a focus on the one true God and like us were easily distracted by false idols. What Jesus did was to name them.

Jesus saw wealth and money as the attractions which pull people away from God and the poor. According to him, such is the power of wealth that it can even become our master and we its slave. The trouble is that there's only room for one master's chair inside us, and that can only be occupied by either God or wealth – the two of them cannot sit on one another's lap.

Jesus met lots of rich people. He was as loving to each of them as he was to the poor, but he didn't pull any punches when it came to telling them the truth. That truth is the same for us today, and it is a double-edged sword: following Jesus means putting all other gods aside, but it also means enjoying a relationship with the

Creator of heaven and earth. I don't think that sounds like such a bad deal.

The story of Jesus meeting the rich young man pulls into focus the power that wealth can have over us. This man was probably a member of the ruling Sanhedrin, certainly young and definitely rich. He was also genuinely interested in finding out about the secret to eternal life, falling to his knees as he approached Jesus (Mark 10:17).

In response to this question, Jesus showed that what he meant by keeping the commandments and what the rich young man meant were two different things. He homed in on the bits of the law that deal with relationships with other people as opposed to how we obey God, and offered the young man a crystal clear explanation of what 'love your neighbour' meant for him. It was too much to take, and as the man walked back to his riches, Jesus reminded his disciples how hard it is to serve two masters. By telling him to sell up and give everything to the poor, Jesus also reminds us that choosing to follow him is a major decision, but with a major reward. Once he had sold up, the rich young man wasn't going to be left hanging around; Jesus offered him the chance of following him, the chance to become his friend.

No examination of God's idea of failure would be complete without looking at some of the more fiery passages in the Bible. There are times when, no matter how much they professed their faith or executed religious rituals, God's anger could not be withheld from his people. The reason was nearly always the same: neglect of the poor and oppressed.

It's really quite simple. God wants it *all* – no hold-backs or crossed-fingers, just the plain honest truth of a phrase like 'God, I'm going to try to follow your lead'. But what does that mean? We've sussed out that the poor are way up on God's list of priorities, and that success in God's book means obedience, sacrifice and relationship while failure comes in the form of altered allegiances and hypocrisy, but still there's the question as to how we do it.

The first inquisitive step might take you to

the Bible, settling on the life of Jesus. We all know the facts about his life: poverty, sacrifice, unconditional love and death. He changed the rules and performed radical acts while at drinking wells, talking to tax collectors and spending time with women and children. Wells, tax, women and children: perhaps not the clearest mission statement that we could adopt for ourselves.

Dig a little deeper and you find three of the Gospels giving space over to the time when 'Jesus talks about the future' on the Mount of Olives. We've looked at Matthew 25 a couple of times already, but the knockout punch at the end of the talk (verse 46) brings it all home. This passage is hot on the heels of different analogies pointing to the importance of being ready for an important event. Perhaps these illustrations of bridegrooms and masters are a little too subtle, for Jesus finally weighs in with 'When the Son of Man comes in his glory . . .' So we're talking judgement day here – the end of the test when it's time to hand in our papers.

It's not about songs, cash or fame. Heck, it's not even about who knows the most memory verses or who has managed to notch up the most conversions. It's about the poor and how we respond to them. Jesus picks some glaringly obvious examples – unusually obvious for one so keen on parable and analogy – feeding, clothing, housing, caring, supporting. Add it all together and what do you get? Lifestyle. It's about how we live.

God has been bringing this point home to us for a long time. Through the prophet Isaiah he declared that the religious trimmings are not what he's after if they are not backed up by the basics of releasing the oppressed, feeding the hungry, giving shelter to the poor and clothes to the naked.

Exploitation, selfishness and greed: these were the Israelites' blind spots back then when Isaiah was in the hot seat. What about us? Where do we slip up? I believe there are three areas that could do with a bit of an honest appraisal from each of us. Here goes.

First up is the fact that we think about Christianity in terms of just believing stuff. Let me explain. It was 3.27 a.m. and I had been awake for hours. I was going to be grumpy the next day if I didn't get to sleep fast. While the prospect of having an excuse for not talking to people and playing solitaire all day wasn't an unattractive one, I knew that my computer was broken. The prospect of being tired, grumpy and without distraction was too much. Sleep was the only answer.

I crept downstairs and took a good long look at the bookshelf. Selecting the most mind-numbingly tedious tome that I could find, I sat down and prepared to read myself into a coma. My medicine that night was the *Lion Handbook to Christian History*. Unfortunately, instead of it resulting in me dribbling into my slippers within seconds, I found the whole thing totally absorbing, particularly the bits around 400 AD. It seems that at about that time the Roman Emperer Constantine became a Christian. Suddenly the faith was OK, cool even. According to Mr Lion, up until then Christianity had been a very different affair, with persecutions and

---

Top Tips for the Upwardly Mobile
have a designer label fast with your friends —
avoid wearing any logos for a weekend

torture very much on the daily menu for a follower of Christ. In the days prior to Constantine's conversion, it said, Christians were known by their behaviour. After this point they became known by whether they signed up to a set of beliefs. In other words, when it had been an underground movement and the victim of persecution, Christianity was made up of people who behaved differently. Later, Christians were recognised by what they said, which usually was about as profoundly fluffy and insightful as 'Oh yes, I'm a Christian too. Isn't it *super*?'

Are things so very different today? I grew up in a church which faithfully taught me the stories of the Bible, for which I am grateful. It taught me about good doctrine, and for that too I am grateful. When it came to how to apply those two strands, however, the church was strangely silent. You see, we've got to learn how to live Christianity and not just believe it. Of course this is nothing new. How many times have you heard non-Christians slagging the Church off for playing host to hypocrisy? It's a fair cop; we say all these things that we believe, but when it comes to acting on them . . .

'How can you say you believe?' asked James. 'You say you have faith, I'll show you my faith by how I live.' If we can't show people our faith

Problems and Solutions

OK, so lifestyle matters. You've sussed out the link between what we buy in the shop and the lives of the people who made them. You know that there are more than a few profit-centred companies out there who like to slash their overheads and increase their margins by employing cheap labour. The real trouble is that the word 'cheap' can also be taken to mean 'easily exploited' or 'too poor to make a fuss about dangerous working conditions'. You see, it happens, and just because we might tut-tut and declare that it's a real shocker, if we buy their goods, we justify their methods. Is it going too far to say that we have blood on our hands? Well, if someone dies making those gorgeous trainers of ours – and believe me, it happens – perhaps in some way we do.

So what's the solution? Go around in

nothing but a home-made cotton thong? Probably best not, all things considered, but that's not the end of it. There's something called Fair Trade, a system designed to ensure that the product you buy has been produced ethically. That means that the workers were paid a decent wage and given decent conditions. Right now you can find the Fair Trade logo on tea and coffee as well as a few other notables. This is a great start, but it needs to go further, with clothing and electronics manufacturers joining in, to name but two.

This is where you can make a difference: why not write to the manufacturers of your favourite goods and ask them about their manufacturing policies; if they make their stuff overseas (and many companies do), is it all kosher? Tell them you'll boycott their goods and buy elsewhere until the situation is put right. Get your mates to join in too. It's all a matter of numbers; if enough purchasers make a big enough noise, most profit-led big boys will toe the line.

by how it changes our lives, then perhaps we don't really have faith after all. Perhaps what we have is little more than silhouettes and masquerades.

Here's the second one. It's not just enough to experience the stuff. We all know people who are meetings junkies, fuelled up on big-time summer and Easter festivals, topped up with Sunday meetings, and just plain miserable in between.

Now stick with me for just a minute while I tell you about where I come from. It's a kind of small town called Amersham, and like most small towns it has an annual fair. There are stalls where people old enough to remember the last world war try to recreate it by doing battle over who has the best marrow/cabbage/marmalade. There are young people who try their best to impress their mates by pretending to smoke while at the same time feeling petrified that mum or dad will see them, and there's a bloke operating the squealing PA from a caravan in which he has been locked for some considerable amount of time with only a crate of beer and an increasingly intense desire to burp/say hello to his mates/sing the theme tune to *Titanic*. There are drum

---

Top Tips for the Upwardly Mobile
do something secret and good

majorettes, cubs, scouts, guides, even a delegation from the local Ex Polish Servicemen's/Cheap Beer and Fags Club. It's great.

Within a ten-mile radius of Amersham there are at least five churches with over 600 members in each. There are probably about another fifteen or twenty slightly smaller charismatic evangelical churches as well as a whole load more from across the spectrum of the Church. And how many were at Amersham fair? None. Not one. Zilch. Keine. All these amazing places with fired-up-super-turbo meetings and not one of them managed to get out and wave the flag alongside the vegetable growers and community groups. They were too busy with their training courses, healing meetings and renewal events to get out and be where all the non-Christians that Jesus loves were.

That sort of thing sends out a message that the Church will talk to people but only if the people go to the Church. Neutral ground doesn't exist for us in the Church, far less the prospect of 'meeting people where they are at'. Something to be proud of? I think not. We need to break this meeting culture of ours if we are to experience any kind of revival. Any casual reading of the gospel would easily demonstrate that Jesus would have been at Amersham fair that afternoon, hanging out with the people, probably healing them, delivering just the right words to a widow and enjoying a few rounds of Pin the Tail on the Donkey (whether or not that would be cheating – bearing in mind that he is omniscient – is perhaps best left for another book altogether). Where were we? Back in the pew learning more about the theory.

Finally we need to go beyond private behaviour. What I mean is this: my discipleship as a young Christian growing up in my church basically taught me that to be a good follower of Jesus I had to not smoke, not drink, not take drugs and only have sex with the right person. If I kept it up for a couple of decades I'd probably make it to be a deacon or an elder. Private behaviour, you see. My church didn't encourage me to think about issues like whom I should work for, how I could be involved in the community, how to react to ethical issues or how I should spend my money. One member of the congregation once told me, 'My company's aim is to make money, so when I'm at work my aim is to make money. When I'm at church I'm there to worship God.' He said it without irony.

Is that the limit of Christianity? Does it not have any place in the work environment? Does it only relate to our personal morality? Important as personal morality is, I have to reply that no, Christianity is about far more than just us. Get back to Isaiah 58; see how it rams home the message that we have to get beyond issues of personal holiness and plough ahead into the realms of justice, politics and community. Making money, running a business, town planning, they're all issues about which God has plenty to say. He created all those worlds in the first place, and to write him off as being irrelevant to those areas is a grave mistake. If we want to hook up with some Almighty Revival we simply have to get it into our heads that Christianity is about *everything*.

God gave other practical nuggets of advice for ways in which we might be able to sort ourselves out with some lifestyle integrity. In Leviticus 25 there's the suggestion that every fifty years the land should return to the original owner. Over the course of time, illness, bereavement or a lack of ability may lead some families to become poorer than others, but the year of Jubilee prevents the gap between rich and poor from ever growing too wide. After all, the earth is ultimately God's anyway, so who are we to grumble about what's ours and not theirs? Aren't we really just the stewards of the earth, the resident caretakers?

We've already seen that when Jesus called his disciples to sign up for the ride, it didn't necessarily mean saying goodbye to all forms of money, personal wealth or support. Instead the disciples stopped pursuing the gain of wealth for themselves while they were with Jesus. As you stand on the verge of a career, you have some choices to make too. I'm not talking about deciding between 'serving the Lord' or getting a 'proper' job; your lifestyle can be equally radical and effective in a huge range of jobs. Those decisions are for another time and place but, for now, you can decide that, whatever your career, you will give yourself the best chance of having a lifestyle that will help you follow Jesus's lead.

Interaction

- Read Mark 12:41–4. Apart from the fact that Jesus blew her cover, the widow was doing a fantastic bit of Secret Service. How good are you at keeping secrets just between yourself and God? Try one today.

- Jesus makes it clear what the Father will be looking for. Refresh your memory by giving Matthew 25:31–46 a quick look over. Do you get any sense that Jesus thinks there are any other factors that will be taken into consideration when it's time to divide the sheep from the goats?

- There's a concept called Progressive Tithing, which means giving away more cash the more you earn. For example, once you've set a base figure to be tithed at 10 per cent, any extra £1000 increases in income are accompanied by 5 per cent increases in giving. Others – like John Wesley – opt for setting themselves a financial ceiling – all money earned above that figure would be given away. Talk about these two ideas. Which one would you go for? Are you prepared to sign up for it right now?

There is a danger that in defining Christianity as a set of rules we miss out on the heart that lies behind it, much like the rich young man. Let's be honest here: leading a sacrificial life is hard work, and we need support throughout. That's why, in proclaiming the vital importance of action, it's equally vital that we don't forget the necessity of relationship. Like Jesus, we too are dependent on the Father for support, strength and power. In the middle of all the *doing*, Jesus spent time alone with the Father in prayer and simple presence, and our needs today are no different from his back then.

But, kind of sneakily, God has made sure that relationship and action are baked together in one life-changing pie. Turning back to Isaiah 58, it's clear that the passage falls into three sections. First up is the reality of the present situation: the fact that there is a lack of interplay between the Israelites' words and their deeds. Next comes the positive statement about what God *does* want: a choice blend of religious activity and loving lifestyle. Finally, God delivers the treat: if this gets done – if God's people finally do suss out

the way to be true with words as well as actions –
then their 'light will rise in the darkness' and they
'will rebuild ancient ruins'. In short, it's revival –
the move of God that many in the Church have
been looking for over the last few years. Most
agree that revival hasn't come yet. Perhaps now
we know why.

The following is a project of Tearfund and Viz-A-Viz
in association with Christians in Sport:

GO2H – Game of 2 Halves
Just do something –
it could change your world

THE GAME

Life treats people differently
It is estimated that in the developing world over
40,000 young people are dying each day. Why?
Because of choices:

We can choose the latest replica shirt
In the developing world many young people have
no access to basic, life saving healthcare.

We can pay to go to the leisure centre
In the developing world many young people
cannot afford to pay to go to school and are
denied the education that will teach them how
to stay alive.

We can pay per view
In the developing world many are forced to watch

life pass by without the opportunities for something better.

In the game of life the two halves are far from being equal

GO2H puts you in the driving seat, straps you in and tells you that you can make a difference. It's not about being the best, leaving it to the pros or sitting back and watching on the box: **GO2H** is about getting involved. If you think it's unfair that others face a tougher and shorter life just because of where they were born, then you have an option to **just do something**.

GO2H is an opportunity to raise money by doing something that you enjoy: sport. In fact, even if the prospect of doing sport brings to mind images of drizzly cross country runs and scary games teachers, **GO2H** is still for you. It's not about who raises the most, it's about being part of the team.

HOW DOES IT WORK?

GO2H is an opportunity for you to put on an event – any event – to raise money. Tearfund will then pass the money on to projects working with young people throughout the developing world, helping to provide healthcare, education and life skills where it really counts.

GO2H can be done solo or in a group. You could raise the cash by getting sponsored to play a sport or attempt a sporting challenge. You could charge people to play sport or even to watch it. If you were up for it, you could try putting on a whole range of tournaments and events to raise the profile, or you could even use **GO2H** alongside a school sports day, raising money along the way.

It's easy to do and there's no limit to how far you could take it. There are no weird offside rules, complex game plans or league structures; it's as simple as you want it to be. **Just do something**.

WHAT NEXT?

If you're keen there are two packs that will tell you more and provide all you need to play the game.

1. Sporting handbook

This is the basic version that gives it to you plain and simple. It's *free* and tells you all you need to know to join in. There are useful sponsorship forms as well as handy hints and plenty of background information to make sure that you're fully warmed up when it comes to the big day.

2. Complete manual

This version costs £9.99, but includes everything you need to put on a storming **GO2H** event. There's a video that tells you more (great for getting people motivated), teaching resources, an Olympic quiz, as well as bags of ideas and tips for putting on an event and details of sports that will give an extra flavour to your fundraising.

To order a pack call 0845 355 8355 or check out our website at www.GO2H.org